Most saltwate
Here are som

- Scale the fish (a spoon works great for this)
- Slit the fish from the vent to the chin
- Remove entrails and gills (head if preferred)
- Make several shallow slits across each side
- Rub salt, pepper, and spices of your choice into the slits
- Rub cooking oil on both sides of the fish
- Cook on a hot, well-oiled grill until the fish has an internal temperature of at least 145 degrees Fahrenheit

DAVE'S TIPS

Equipment

- Occasionally run your leader through your fingers; if it is rough, change it.

- After a snag, check your hook. Modern hooks are very sharp, but the points are brittle.

- Put plastic beads on each side of sliding weights to protect your knots.

Fishing

- Freshen your cut bait every 15 to 20 minutes to keep maximum scent in the water. The same is good advice for "Gulp" style plastic baits too: Resoak them.

- Use large cut baits and ignore the tap-tap of small fish and wait for the strong tug from larger fish.

- You'll generally be more successful when targeting a specific species.

- If plagued by bait robbers or catfish, fish a little deeper or move a few yards. Large fish often hang out at the edge or just below schools of small fish.

Your Catch

- Taste is often improved by bleeding large fish soon after they are caught. Stun the fish, and then cut or remove the gills to do this.

- Fillets kept in salt water (not fresh water) will be moister when cooked.

- The key to good-tasting fish is keeping them cool and eating them as soon as possible.

SURF & PIER FISHING

THE GEAR, TIPS, AND TECHNIQUES TO GET STARTED

Dave Bosanko

Adventure Skills Guides

CATCH SALTWATER FISH LIKE A PRO

Adventure Skills Guides

The inshore waters along our coast are some of the most productive waters in the U.S. and are great fun to fish. Many offshore fish cruise these waters in search of prey, making the chance of a trophy catch possible, even close to shore. Much of this coastal water is accessible from shore and is easy and economical to fish, even for beginners. If you have a basic understanding of fishing but don't often fish, or you have only fished freshwater, this guide will help you start successfully fishing in saltwater, whether it's from a pier, a jetty, or from a beach.

This guide assumes you have at least a basic understanding of fishing and fishing tackle. If you are new to fishing, pick up *Freshwater Fishing*; it will quickly get you started. With both guides in hand, you will soon be catching fish along the coast like a pro.

DAVE BOSANKO

Dave Bosanko is an avid fisherman and naturalist with degrees in Biology and Chemistry from the University of Kansas. He spent a long career at the University of Minnesota's field stations before retiring. In addition to fishing, he enjoys hiking, sailing, and building small wooden boats. Much of his time is now spent writing or visiting natural areas in the U.S. and beyond.

Cover and book design by Jonathan Norberg
Edited by Brett Ortler

All illustrations by Jonathan Norberg except:
Steve Jones: cinch knots, 17; Anthony Hertzel: jetty fishing, 22 and channel, 26

Cover image: **bartuchna@yahoo.pl/shutterstock.com**

All images copyrighted.

Used under license from Shutterstock.com:
anant thong: 5c; **Brent Hofacker:** back gatefold; **ESB Professional:** 6 main; **Gary Paul Lewis:** 22 main; **I like to take pictures:** 12 main; **IRINA ORLOVA:** 4 main; **juliasabs:** 21 main; **Ken Schulze:** 18 main; **Khairil Azhar Junos:** inside gatefold; **Ihorib:** 3a; **Gena Melendrez:** 3 main; **Mikhail Anikaev:** 15 main; **mooremedia:** 20a; **MRomanPhotography:** 4a; **Norm Lane:** 5a; **nyker:** 8a; **Real Window Creative:** 5b; **Shoot66Studio:** 8b; **Volodymyr Maksymchuk:** 10 main; **Zadaorozhnyi Viktor:** 7a; **zezamm:** 9a

10 9 8 7 6 5 4 3 2 1

Surf & Pier Fishing: The Gear, Tips, and Techniques to Get Started
Copyright © 2021 by Dave Bosanko
Published by Adventure Publications, an imprint of AdventureKEEN
310 Garfield Street South, Cambridge, Minnesota 55008
(800) 678-7006
www.adventurepublications.net
All rights reserved
Printed in China
ISBN 978-1-64755-048-6

You don't need tons of fancy gear to get started fishing; you might have what you need already!

This guide will help you select the right equipment, rig your lines, choose the best bait, find a good spot to fish, and stay safe. It also includes a special section, "Dave's tips," with tried-and-true advice to help you catch more fish.

It is organized so you can quickly find the information you need to get started fishing. We will first cover some safety tips, then subjects common to most saltwater shore fishing, and at the back specific information for pier, jetty, and surf fishing. In the common section, topics that are more applicable to just one kind of fishing will be highlighted; blue for pier, green for jetty, and orange for surf fishing.

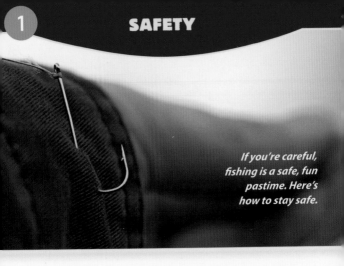

If you're careful, fishing is a safe, fun pastime. Here's how to stay safe.

Being mindful of your surroundings and what you're doing will not only keep you safe, it will also help you catch fish, and enjoy your trip to the coast. Here are some safety tips to keep in mind.

Don't Get Burned—Sunburns can be painful and can spoil a trip, but long-term sun exposure can be deadly. Put on sunscreen and cover up. If you wear long pants on a sunny beach for protection don't forget your bare ankles. Reflection off the sand can burn them.

DAVE'S TIP: Keep sunscreen off your bait, it doesn't taste good to people and probably doesn't to fish either.

Don't Get Hooked—Hooks are sharp, and saltwater hooks are often large. Circle hooks are great for hooking and holding fish, but they do just as well on people.

Don't Fall In—Piers are often crowded, and pier fishing is relatively safe, but some piers are in locations where the ocean can be violent. Most piers, but not all, have guardrails, and many are high above the water. Keep your feet firmly on the deck. Don't climb over the rail to fish the pilings or to land a fish. If you do fall in it may be hard to get back to shore and out of the water.

Jetties are made for water control, not for walking. Most are made of large rocks, so mist and splashing waves make them slippery and very hard to walk on or climb onto if you fall off. Wear good shoes.

Rough surf can be hard to stand up in. Be sure your footing is sound before you attempt a long cast. If you are wearing waders, be sure they are belted off at the top so they won't fill with water if you fall. Know your beach. A good fishing beach at low tide may be a slippery rock and a wall at high tide. Always check the tide tables before you go.

Don't Get Sick—Most fish are safe to eat, but pollutants in the food chain are a valid concern. In addition, some ocean fish are seasonally toxic due to ciguatera poisoning. Check your state's health department websites for updates.

Before your excursion, make sure you have a fishing license and are familiar with the fishing regulations/catch limits in your area.

Licenses and Catch Limits—Many states require a separate fishing license for salt water, and most saltwater fish are now regulated by both size and season. When you stop by the sporting goods store to get your license, pick up the current regulations and a field guide to help identify your catch if you want to take some fish home.

Smartphone Apps—Most of us will be taking our smartphones when we head out fishing. Rather than checking your email while waiting for a bite, you might as well use it to help you when you're out fishing. There are lots of good fishing apps available, and I am only going to list a few of them. The best apps are the ones you actually use, not the ones you have on your phone because you think they are cool.

Weather Underground: A good weather app that includes wind and barometric pressure forecast, but there are many other options.

Fishing Rules: You will need some way to check on local regulations. This app uses your location to give you the size and catch limit for any fish you catch in any state, just by clicking on the fish. It even has pictures if you don't recognize your catch.

Navionics: You need to check on the tides when you are coastal fishing. This app will give the tide tables or tide schedules when you click on your location and so much more. Designed primarily for navigation, it will also show you the bottom structure at your coastal location as well as in your favorite lake or river back home.

Google Earth: By looking at close-ups of your fishing spot at several different times of day it is often possible to see underwater structures that could hold fish. This can be very helpful if you are fishing at high tide and want to know what your fishing spot looks like at low tide.

BASIC FISHING GEAR AND EQUIPMENT

Your fishing tackle does not have to be big or expensive for you to enjoy fishing along our coastal shores. Expensive equipment doesn't catch more fish. That big snook that was just hooked down the pier was not swimming along waiting to be caught by an expensive rod. Good equipment may last longer and cause less trouble, but don't stay home because you don't have the best stuff. It is knowledge and the amount of time you spend fishing that provides the best results.

There is a difference between freshwater and saltwater tackle, but it is not all about size. There are a lot more small fish in the ocean than large ones, and most of the fish you will be catching along the coast will weigh less than ten pounds. What's more, most of the best-eating fish will be well under five pounds. Many a fine meal has been made from a stringer of pan-size fish caught from under a pier. It takes heavy equipment to land the biggest coastal fishes, but not most of the inshore fish. So, yes your freshwater fishing gear will work just fine at the coast, but there are some things to keep in mind when fishing in saltwater.

Ocean salt is corrosive and damaging, even for saltwater tackle. Freshwater equipment brought to the coast for a day of fishing is even more susceptible to damage from salt. Surf fishing has the added hazard of getting sand in the gears of your reel. Take a jug of fresh water with you to the beach so you can rinse off a reel that falls in the sand. Make sure to keep the mechanical parts of your tackle clean and well greased. It is a good idea to wash all of your rods and reels in freshwater when you get home. Believe it or not, taking them with you into the shower (with no hooks attached!) works well.

 DAVE'S TIP: Size your equipment to the average fish you expect to catch. It is a lot more fun catching fish than it is spending your time watching over-sized tackle just so you will be able to land that six-foot shark if it comes by.

Rods—There are rods designed to cover almost every situation you can think of in coastal fishing. There are short, stiff rods that can lift a heavy fish up to a high pier, very long rods that can cast a hundred yards into the surf, and everything in between. But by keeping a few things in mind you can select one or two rods that will cover most of your needs.

When fishing on the coast, the length of your fishing rod isn't as important as its sturdiness. Between tides, currents, and wind, coastal waters are always moving, and frequently the most violently moving water is often the most productive. This means that the terminal tackle for coastal fishing is often heavy, with three- to four- ounce sinkers, and big plugs or heavy jigs. To handle casting this amount of weight, coastal rods need to be relatively stiff.

Longer rods have more leverage and thus can cast longer distances. This can be a real advantage when surf fishing but can be a disadvantage, and even a hazard, when fishing a crowded pier. Even in the surf a long rod is not always an advantage, as many of the most desirable fish feed just out from where the waves break on the beach. A stiff seven-foot rod is a good choice for pier and jetty fishing and a ten-foot surf rod is a good overall choice for the beach.

 DAVE'S TIP: Choose a rod with a good, long handle. It will help you cast heavy terminal tackle, and sticking the handle between your legs or under your arm will give you more power and control when landing big fish.

Reels—The two most commonly used reels for coastal fishing are bait-casting reels and open-faced spinning reels. Closed spinning reels tend to capture corrosive saltwater and sand inside the housing, and it can be hard to clean out, so such reels are not often used at the ocean. Spinning reels are a little easier to use and a little more trouble-free than bait-casting reels, but both work well for coastal fishing. Spinning reels have a slight advantage over bait-casting reels for casting long distances, and so they are the most common reel on the beach.

Any reel you choose should have a deep throat so it can hold a large amount of heavy line. After a long cast you need sufficient line left on the reel to fight a large fish, which may take some distance to turn and land. Two hundred and fifty yards is a good amount to choose. Keep in mind that a reel will hold more braided line than monofilament of the same test weight.

DAVE'S TIP: Consider a bait-runner spinning reel. These reels have a mechanism, which when set, allows a fish to run with the line and not steal your rod. When you turn the crank your drag is engaged to fight the fish.

Line—Both monofilament and braided lines are commonly used in coastal fishing. Monofilament line stretches, absorbing some of the shock when fighting a large fish. Braided line does not stretch, but it does make it easier to feel a bite. Braided line is more flexible and smaller in diameter than the same weight of monofilament line and less likely to kink. It is also much more expensive.

You don't need exceptionally heavy line: 20- to 25- pound test line is adequate to land most coastal fish and heavy, stiff line is often a disadvantage. You will, however, usually need a leader. Use a heavier leader than your main line; this will protect your line from a fish's teeth or sharp rocks, and will be lighter when you are presenting small baits. Fluorocarbon line makes excellent leaders. It is highly abrasion resistant and almost invisible in the water. You will need steel leaders when targeting some some fish, but in general you will be more successful using a monofilament line, like fluorocarbon, for a leader.

DAVE'S TIP: Braided line is much more expensive than monofilament line so on a big reel you may want to back up a hundred and fifty yards of braid with less expensive line.

It's important to match the size of your bait to your hook.

Hooks—There are almost as many hook styles as fish in the ocean. The main difference between saltwater and freshwater hooks is that for the same size, saltwater hooks are generally made of heavier gauge wire.

If you are fishing for larger species, be sure to upgrade to heavy hooks that won't get straightened out. Hook shape is not as important as size, but hooks must be sharp. Many saltwater fish have very hard mouths. In most situations circle hooks should be considered. These hooks hold fish well and usually lodge in the corner of the mouth making it easy to release fish with little injury.

 DAVE'S TIP: Match the hook to the size of your bait. The point should go through the bait and be exposed with a little room left in the bend.

Circle hook with cut bait

Sinkers—Sinkers come in many weights and shapes, all with the job of keeping your bait where you want it. Heavy sinkers are the rule in the always-moving coastal waters, but shape is important too. One- to four ounce-sinkers are sufficient for most coastal fishing. In general, you will be most successful using the least amount of weight possible.

The three most common sinker shapes used in coastal fishing are the pyramid, the egg, and the bank, each with their own advantages and disadvantages. Egg sinkers are designed to roll around in the water for a more natural bait presentation, and they slide on your line allowing a fish to run with the bait without feeling the sinker's weight. Eggs are the most popular coastal fishing sinker and can be rigged in many different ways. Pyramid sinkers are blocky with flat sides and are good to use in the sifting sands of the surf. Pyramids easily hang up in crevices so are not good to use in the rocks. Bank sinkers look a little like bullets and are not as common as the other two, but they are not as likely to get caught in the rocks. They also hold pretty well in the surf.

 DAVE'S TIP: Sputnik sinkers are oval, lead sinkers with protruding wires that hold well in the sandy surf but fold back when you retrieve them.

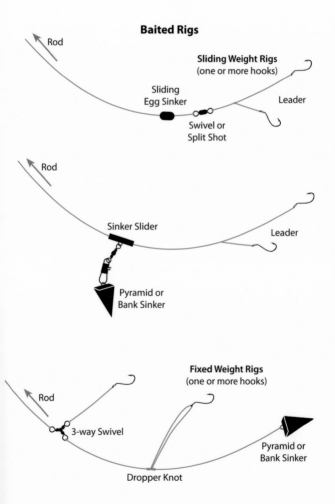

Baited Rigs

Rod

Sliding Weight Rigs
(one or more hooks)

Sliding
Egg Sinker

Leader

Swivel or
Split Shot

Rod

Sinker Slider

Leader

Pyramid or
Bank Sinker

Fixed Weight Rigs
(one or more hooks)

Rod

3-way Swivel

Pyramid or
Bank Sinker

Dropper Knot

Natural, locally caught bait is best.

NATURAL BAIT

The best natural bait is live and locally caught; it's what the fish around you are eating. Fresh dead local bait is the next-best option. Frozen bait will catch most fish, but it tends to be a little softer than fresh bait and harder to keep on the hook; this is especially true with shrimp. Ask around a little to see what is working.

Shrimp—A big live shrimp is the favorite food of most coastal fish but a whole dead shrimp or a piece of one is often just as good.

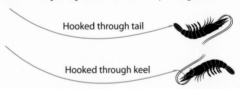

Hooked through tail

Hooked through keel

Fish—Live active small fish make wonderful bait, but a dead one or piece of one (cut bait) works well too. Cut bait is inexpensive, always available, and probably the most commonly used bait along the coast. Cutting up a fresh fish you have just caught is the best. Using a Sabiki rig, you can often catch your bait from a pier or jetty.

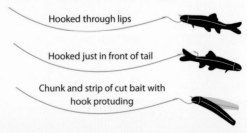

Hooked through lips

Hooked just in front of tail

Chunk and strip of cut bait with hook protuding

DAVE'S TIP: When cutting up bait fish, fillet both sides of a small fish from tail to gills leaving the fillets attached at the gills. The bait is now a head, backbone, and tail with sides that flap with the waves.

Crabs and Sand Fleas—Small crabs and sand fleas are excellent bait when you can get them. Large blue crabs, if cut up, work well too. You can catch your own crabs and sand fleas or you can purchase them at the bait shop. You can get blue crabs from your local fishmonger.

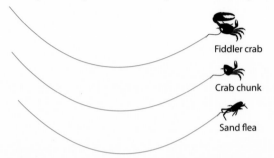

Fiddler crab

Crab chunk

Sand flea

Squid—Squid is excellent saltwater bait (sold in grocery stores as calamari). Unlike many other baits it is tough and not easily picked off your hook by small fish. Depending on the squid's size and what you're fishing for, you can fish the whole squid, just the head, or a single tentacle. The body is most commonly cut into strips.

Marine Worms (sandworms, bloodworms, and clamworms)— Marine worms are popular baits in some parts of the country, but they are not as commonly used in the South or along the Gulf Coast. But wherever you are, they work well when you can get them.

2 hooks

Clumped on hook

NOTE: Marine worms have legs

ARTIFICIAL BAITS

Lures are very effective in coastal waters, but are more commonly used in the surf rather than on piers and jetties. On the beach you can move around in order to cover different water. On piers and jetties, you fish the same water repetitively, waiting for fish to come by. If you're using a lure on a pier, be sure to work your lure around each of the pilings. When using fishing lures from a jetty, the quieter water between the jetty and the beach is good place to try.

Jigs—Jigs are great lures to use from piers and on the beach; they are a little hard to use on jetties, as they often snag in the rocks. Jigs are typically fished on or near the bottom with a hop-and-wait retrieval.

In most coastal situations three quarter- to one-ounce jigs will work fine, but if the water is deep with a strong current, you will need a heavier one to stay on the bottom. In the still water at harbor piers small quarter-ounce jigs are very effective. Jigs are often tipped with some kind fresh bait to make them more attractive. Scented plastic baits like Gulp! products work well when added to jigs. In rocky areas jigs are often fished suspended below a float.

 DAVE'S TIP: Suspending a jig tipped with a tasty squid tentacle just over the rocks is very effective. (See the rigs section). In the surf, a good technique is to drag your jig in the sand a little just before you hop it. The small sand cloud this makes looks like a crab or small fish making a break for it.

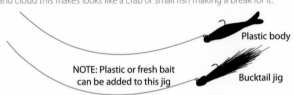

Plastic body

NOTE: Plastic or fresh bait can be added to this jig

Bucktail jig

Plugs and Spoons—Floating or diving plugs and spoons can all be effective lures when coastal fishing. Under the right conditions, plugs and spoons are most commonly used when surf fishing, but they can occasionally be effective around piers and jetties and often in the protected waters on the backside of jetties.

 **DAVE'S TIP:** In the surf, cast plugs into the flat water between the breaking waves. Fish spoons close the bottom, stirring up sand now and then.

In general, saltwater lures are bigger and have stronger hooks than freshwater lures, but they look the same and are fished in the same way.

Many freshwater lures do just as well in saltwater as they do in freshwater. In rough water, it is often helpful to add a small cone-shaped sliding sinker in front of your plug.

Plastic Baits—The new scented plastic baits, like Gulp!, are very effective in saltwater. These baits feel natural and taste good enough so fish do not spit them out as readily as they would other artificial baits. They come in many shapes and colors and can be used the same way you would use natural bait. They may seem expensive at first, but remember: they don't rot and can be stored.

 DAVE'S TIP: Exchange plastic baits often putting the used ones back in the jar to resoak them.

There are about as many ways to rig a rod as there are fish in the sea. Here are a few tips!

BOTTOM RIGS

There are hundreds of ways to attach hooks, sinkers, floats, and lures to your line. They all are designed to keep your bait in front of the fish and entice them to eat it. Here are a few basic configurations to get you started.

Slip sinker, river

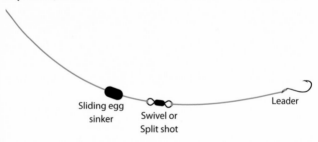

Sliding egg sinker

Swivel or Split shot

Leader

End sinker, Sabiki

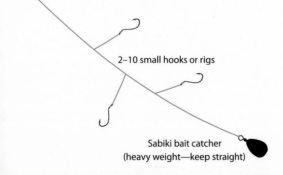

2–10 small hooks or rigs

Sabiki bait catcher
(heavy weight—keep straight)

FLOAT RIGS

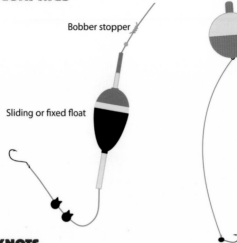

Bobber stopper

Sliding or fixed float

Jig

KNOTS

Tying good fishing knots is important in all kinds of fishing. Fishing lines are slippery when wet, and all knots lower the test weight of your line. Good knots help with both of these problems. In coastal fishing you will need to know how to tie at least two basic kinds of knots: one to attach things to the end of your line and one to attach two lines when you want to use a leader. Here are three basic knots that will get you started.

Uni-Knot (for attaching two lines)

Circle blue line six
times and pull snug

Circle orange line six
times and pull snug

Slide knot

Slide knot

Pull knot together

Dropper Loop (for a standoff hook or sinker)

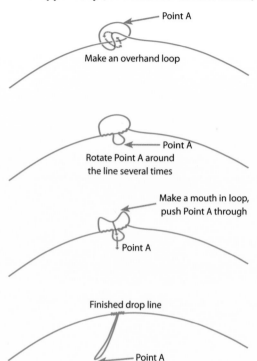

Point A

Make an overhand loop

Point A

Rotate Point A around
the line several times

Make a mouth in loop,
push Point A through

Point A

Finished drop line

Point A

Cinch Knot (for terminal tackle)

1

Start by passing the line
through the eyelet of your
hook or lure.

2

Wrap the end of the line around
the main line five times.

3

Bring the end of the line
throught the loop just above
the eye and then back through
the new loop next to the coils.

4

Wet the line and pull the knot
tight; clip off the excess.

With bait and sometimes even rental gear available, piers are often a no-hassle fishing option.

There are a lot of piers along our coast that are great places to fish. Many areas have specifically constructed fishing piers, some with food and bait available on site. Other fishing piers are abandoned bridges that are now open for fishing, or short pieces of dock that you may be able to get permission to fish from. Some of these piers are very productive, and others not so much, but most structures built out into the water will attract some fish during some part of the day. At the local bait shop, ask about public piers, the best time to fish, and what folks are using for bait.

Special Equipment—You will not need too much extra equipment to fish from a pier, but there are a lot of things that make it easier. Look around to see what other anglers are using on the pier. The one thing you will need to figure out is how to land a fish that is too heavy to lift with your line. Walking your fish to the shore is sometimes possible, but a round crab net on a stout line is a better tactic. Often there will be someone near by that will help you out.

When—The general rule of coastal fishing is that a rising tide (flood tide) or a falling tide (ebb tide) is better fishing than the time between tides (slack tide). This mostly holds true for piers; however, there are fish that live and feed around the pier pilings that are always present. Some short piers in shallow water may only be productive at high tide. Many crabs and baitfish are more active in the dark so fishing at night can be very productive. Lighted piers in shallow water may yield good catches at night, but nothing during the day.

Where—Your fishing location on the pier is as important as when to fish. If you're targeting open-water fish, choose a spot where the water is much deeper or near the end of the pier, if there's a channel present. On piers that run out through the surf, the first third of the pier is often the best place to be. Fish travel up and down the beach in troughs that form along the beach line. Drop your line between the breaking waves in these troughs. On short, shallow water piers, high tide may be the only time fish are present.

If it is a long pier and you are not having any luck, move around a little and see if it helps. The pier pilings are always good places to try.

Potential Pier Fishing Locations

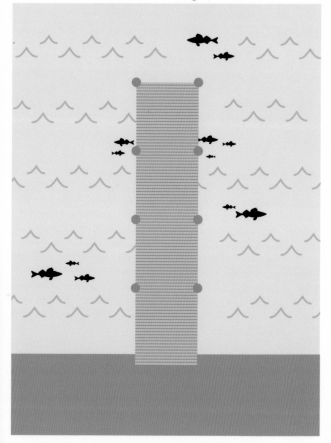

Rigs and Lures—Bottom bait fishing is by far the most common way to fish from a pier; the most common rig is the "fish finder rig"; a sliding egg sinker with a leader. The sinker should be light enough to roll around with the waves but not wander so far that it entangles your neighbor's line. If you are fishing the surf line, a drop line and a pyramid sinker may work better. The most common lures used on piers are jigs, and these are fished around the pilings.

Bridge fishing is much like pier fishing, but traffic is a real concern, so be mindful of your surroundings and safety. If you're fishing with bait, fish with the current pulling the bait away from the bridge, not back under it. Fish avoid bright light so fishing the bridge's shadow line is a good bet. If you're fishing with lures, cast into the current. Fish normally swim with the current, not against it. Mimic this by casting into the current and retrieving back to the bridge slightly faster than the current.

If they are accessible, jetties can be a great option, but use common sense before venturing out onto one.

Jetties are often built at a channel mouth to control water flow, or to protect a harbor. They are typically built of large rocks that provide lots of nooks and crannies that house crabs and small fish. These man-made structures are a great place to fish if you can get out on them. Because they are not designed to be walked upon, they can be dangerous. Some have good flat tops that are easy to traverse, but many are wet, slippery boulder fields. Be mindful of how the wind and waves will affect your return to shore, and only fish on jetties when it's allowed. A dry sunny jetty at low tide may be a wet obstacle course at high tide. That said, jetties are fish magnets and, if you take care, can be great places to find fish.

Special Equipment—Jetties are often wet, windy places. Be sure you have warm, dry clothes; it's hard to have fun, if you are cold and wet, even if you are catching fish. Wear good shoes; even on flat-topped jetties you will have to work your way down through the rocks to land your fish.

There is no specific tackle that is needed to fish jetties, but keep in mind that you're fishing on a rock pile, so snags are inevitable. Transporting your fishing tackle out over the rocks can be cumbersome, but with a little forethought it can be overcome. Anchoring a fishing rod can be a problem on some jetties so be sure you can scramble back to your rod when you get a bite or a large fish may claim it as its own.

When—Like all costal fishing, tides play an important role in jetty fishing. The jetty structure itself ensures that there are always some fish to be caught at any time of day, but the tides influence when larger predator gamefish come to the jetties to hunt. Many jetties are wave-swept or underwater at high tide. As with other coastal fishing, flowing tides stir things up in the water and are more productive than slack tides.

Where—Jetties are built to disrupt or enhance natural water flow so there are always currents around jetties that are influenced by the tides. Jetties normally have a quieter more-protected side and a more active running-side; each is attractive to different kinds of fish. Wherever there is an abrupt change in the flow of water eddies form, and eddies are always great places to fish. This can be where the water sweeps around the end of the jetty or where the water swirls in corners on the beach-side of the jetty.

DAVE'S TIP: If you find a big rock slab just under the water use a bank sinker and a short leader to position your bait on the rock; fish gleaning the rocks for crabs will find it.

Jetty Fishing

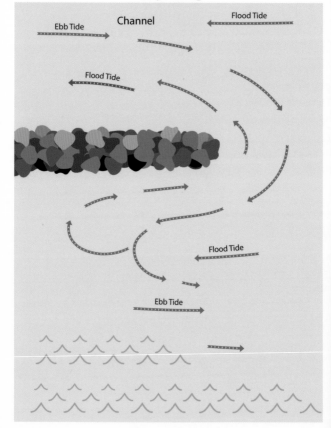

Suspended jig

Rigs and Lures—Bottom fishing with bait is the most common fishing method on jetties, but you will lose some tackle. Bank sinkers attached to the end of the line with drop hooks, or with the sinker on a drop line with a hook on the end will both work well. Using a float rig to keep out of the rocks works well, but your bait needs to be near the bottom. Keep adjusting your fishing depth until you get bites. Jetties are home to lots of crabs, and they are one of the best baits to use amid the rocks.

Floating and diving plugs are good options to use on the quiet side of the jetty. Heavy jigs are effective in the eddies at the end of the jetty. Suspending jigs under floats will help keep them out of the rocks if you want to fish along the edge of the jetty.

 DAVE'S TIP: Attach your sinker with light line or a weak clip so you don't lose your hooks and expensive braided line every time you get snagged.

Fish for small crab or live shrimp with just a split shot for weight where the water is splashing around the big rocks.

Keep an extra rod with a plug or spoon on it handy so if a larger fish chases a school of baitfish to the surface nearby you can cast into it.

Surf fishing has it all: a day at the beach, and the possibility of a free lunch.

There are countless public beaches around our coasts, and they can provide many of exciting fishing opportunities. Like other kinds of fishing it can take years of practice to become an expert surf angler, but with a few basics you can have fun fishing in the surf and catch some fish. In some places, fishing amid the surf means navigating large waves crashing on the rocks; at other beaches, the surf will consist of small waves rolling slowly up on the sand. Always keep your eye on the ocean; the occasional giant wave or big gust of wind may sweep you or your stuff into the water. Extreme surf conditions require specialized tackle and care, but in many cases standard inexpensive equipment will get you successfully fishing from the beach.

Special Equipment—To get started surf fishing you will need little more than a rod and reel and a pocket full of hooks and sinkers. Don't make it complicated. However, there is one piece of equipment that you will need. If you are going to fish with more than one rod (or you want to play volleyball while you fish) you will need some way to keep your rods out of the sand. This is accomplished easily with a sand spike. There are many styles available commercially, but an adequate one can be made by cutting a point on a four-foot piece of 1½" to 2" PVC pipe you get from the hardware store and driving it into the sand.

 DAVE'S TIP: Some of the plastic sand spikes from the bait shop are thin walled and break when pounded into the sand. Some beaches have hard sand, so get a strong one.

When—Tides strongly influence when fish travel and feed. Not only do currents caused by flowing tides stir up the water, dislodging the small creatures that larger fish feed on, high tides allow fish to reach areas unavailable at low tide. It is often debated whether fishing a rising (flood) or falling (ebb) tide is better, but both are definitely better than fishing in between tides (slack tide). In places where the water is very clear, evenings, mornings, and overcast days are often better times to fish than in the bright sun. A warm beach under a full moon is fun fishing and a better-than-average time to catch fish too.

Where—As in all fishing, underwater structure is the key to finding fish, and the surf is no different. The beach around you may look all the same but waves are constantly moving the sand around. You can't see the underwater structure from the beach, but it's there. However, you can see how the waves are breaking and make a good guess at what it looks like under the surface. Entire books have been written on learning to read the surf, but with a few basics you can know enough to catch some fish.

On sandy beaches, the sea bottom is relatively smooth and sandy, and waves run smoothly over deep water and then break as they encounter a shallow sand bar. These bars are constantly changing, forming troughs and pools and occasionally cutting channels running out to sea. These are dangerous for swimmers, but good for fishing. These pools and troughs may be only a few feet deeper than the surrounding water, but that is enough to concentrate fish. In general, the troughs run parallel to the beach and show up as parallel lines of breaking surf. The flat water behind the breaking waves is the deeper water trough that fish travel in when feeding. Any inconsistencies in the breaking waves indicate pools, rocks, or channels, which are good places to try. The first trough may only be a few feet from the beach line or out fifty yards or more, but it is often the most productive place to fish.

The two rules to get you successfully started surf fishing are simple: Fish the deeper water behind the breaking waves and fish any changes in the evenly breaking waves.

Surf Fishing Locations

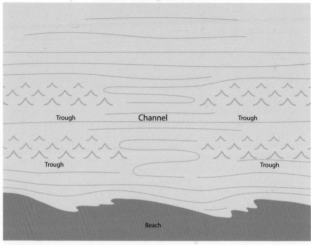

Rigs and Lures—Two to four ounces is usually enough weight to hold your bait in place in normal surf, but at times much more may be needed. The heaver the sinker, the more important it is to use a sliding weight rig so the fish does not feel the weight. Pyramid or sputnik sinkers are good choices for holding in the surf. When fishing for smaller species, multiple hooks above the sinker is the most common arrangement. With bigger baits, a single hook on the end is the way to go. Shortening your leader will make it easier to detect a bite in a rough surf.

Lures can be very effective in the surf. Pull plugs across the quiet water and then through the breaking wave, mimicking an escaping bait fish. Jigs should be heavy enough to stay in contact with the bottom. Spoons are not often used anymore, but they can work great in the surf.

 DAVE'S TIP: Add a jig in front of a large popping plug to simulate a predator chasing a baitfish.

Walk the moonlit beach at night casting a large silver or gold spoon tipped with cut bait into the surf.